SURVIVORS OF THE HOLOCAUST

TRUE STORIES OF SIX EXTRAORDINARY CHILDREN

EDITED BY KATH SHACKLETON   ILLUSTRATED BY ZANE WHITTINGHAM

sourcebooks
eXplore

First published in the United States in 2019 by Sourcebooks

Producer and editor
Kath Shackleton

Contributors
Heinz Skyte
Trude Silman
Martin Kapel
Ruth Rogoff
Arek Hersh
Suzanne Ripton

Illustrations
Zane Whittingham

Design and layout
Ryan Jones

Additional artwork
Laura Tattersfield
Oana Nechifor

Hand-drawn digital illustrations adapted from the original vector-based animation.

Published by Sourcebooks eXplore, an imprint of Sourcebooks Kids
P.O. Box 4410, Naperville, Illinois 60567–4410
(630) 961-3900
sourcebookskids.com

Originally published in 2016 in Great Britain by Franklin Watts, an imprint of Hachette Children's Group, part of the Watts Publishing Group.

Library of Congress Cataloging-in-Publication Data is on file with the publisher.

Source of Production: RR Donnelley Asia Printing Solutions, Ltd.,
Dongguan, Guangdong Province, China
Date of Production: July 2019
Run Number: 5015094

Printed and bound in China.
RRD 10 9 8 7 6 5 4 3 2 1

Foreword

Each story you will read in this book is a true account of what happened to six young people over seventy years ago. Heinz, Trude, Ruth, Martin, Suzanne, and Arek lived at home with their families. They went to school, enjoyed friendships, had hobbies, and hopes for the future. Then one day their lives changed forever. They had done nothing wrong. They were born into Jewish families, and they were persecuted for this reason alone: they were Jewish.

From 1933 onwards, Nazi Germany introduced new anti-Semitic racial measures, which became law in 1935—the Nuremberg Laws. These laws prevented Jewish people from being citizens of Germany and forbade marriage between Jewish and non-Jewish people. Gradually, all their rights were removed.

On the night of November 9th, 1938, synagogues, homes, and businesses owned by Jewish people were attacked and set on fire. This is known as "Kristallnacht," or the Night of Broken Glass. Some thirty thousand Jewish men were arrested and sent to concentration camps. As Nazi Germany occupied the rest of Europe during the Second World War, their racial policies were implemented across the whole of their new territory, including what was then Czechoslovakia, Poland, Holland, Belgium, Greece, Hungary, and France. This led to the Holocaust, during which six million Jewish men, women, and children were systematically murdered.

I have known Trude, Ruth, Martin, Heinz, Arek, and Suzanne for many years. They are an inspiration to people who hear their stories in person. They all lost their country, their families, their culture, and their right to exist simply because they were Jewish.

Today they live in Leeds. They have overcome adversity, made new lives and new families, but they never forget their past. They know they are the lucky ones who escaped or were liberated, but they never forget those who did not.

It is not easy for them to tell their stories. They agreed to because they want people to know what can happen when people are subjected to discrimination and persecution for being seen as "different." Their dearest wish is that no one should suffer as they did and that people should never again stand by when injustice is taking place. It is their belief that we are all part of the human race and we should always respect each other and our differences. We hope by reading these stories, you will be able to think about your own lives and how you can make a difference for a better world today.

Lilian Black

Chair, Holocaust Survivors'
Friendship Association

Contents

HEINZ'S STORY

I REMEMBER THE DAY THAT THE NAZIS CAME TO POWER.

I WAS ALMOST 13.

I REMEMBER LOOKING DOWN FROM OUR WINDOW IN FUERTH, NUREMBERG.

CRACKLE

CRACKLE

CRACKLE

CRACKLE

THE NAZIS ALWAYS CELEBRATED THEIR SUCCESSES BY TORCHLIGHT PROCESSIONS.

AND THEY MARCHED PAST AND SANG SONGS, BLOODTHIRSTY SONGS.

THE NUREMBERG LAWS THAT CAME IN THE AUTUMN OF 1935 LEGALIZED ANTI-JEWISH MEASURES.

Jude

WE WERE NO LONGER ALLOWED TO GO TO CINEMAS AND THEATERS AND BE MEMBERS OF CLUBS.

AS A CHILD OF ANY AGE, TO BE EXCLUDED FROM YOUR PEERS IS A BLOW.

YOU FEEL INFERIOR...

...AND YOU QUESTION YOUR EXISTENCE.

CRACK!

THERE WERE THREE JEWISH BOYS, INCLUDING ME, LEFT IN OUR CLASS.

THE MAIN HITLER YOUTH LEADER CAME AND SAID,

It's time you left the school. We don't want you here!

THUMP!

I LEFT SCHOOL AT 16.

IF IT HADN'T BEEN FOR THE NAZIS, I PROBABLY WOULD HAVE GONE TO UNIVERSITY...

...BUT WE COULD NO LONGER DO THAT, BECAUSE UNIVERSITIES WERE NO LONGER ACCEPTING JEWS.

English

AT THE AGE OF 18, I WENT TO COLLEGE IN HAMBURG TO LEARN ENGLISH.

ONE EVENING, WE HEARD THE NEWS, AND WE KNEW THAT SOMETHING WAS GOING TO HAPPEN.

SO THAT'S WHAT I DID.

I SAT ON PARK BENCHES...

...THEN I WENT AROUND THE DEPARTMENT STORES.

I TRIED TO MAKE MYSELF SMALL, NOT TO STAND OUT.

TAP   CLICK   TAP   TAP

TAP   CLICK   CLICK   TAP

I COULD SEE THE SMOKE FROM THE BURNING SYNAGOGUES EVERYWHERE.

I COULD ALSO SEE GROUPS OF JEWISH PEOPLE BEING FROGMARCHED THROUGH THE STREETS AFTER THEY'D BEEN ARRESTED.

WINDOWS WERE SMASHED.

THE GERMANS INVENTED THE TERM...

KRISTALLNACHT

...BECAUSE OF ALL THE BROKEN GLASS.

EVENTUALLY I WENT HOME. THE LANDLADY SAID, "THE GESTAPO HAVE BEEN LOOKING FOR YOU." IT'S A GOOD THING THAT I DID LEAVE THE DIGS, OTHERWISE I WOULD HAVE BEEN SENT TO A CONCENTRATION CAMP.

FATHER WAS ARRESTED AND THEN SENT TO DACHAU CONCENTRATION CAMP NEAR MUNICH.

HE WAS THERE FOR FIVE OR SIX WEEKS.

MOST OF THE PEOPLE WERE RELEASED JUST BEFORE CHRISTMAS 1938.

FATHER CAME HOME AND WAS A COMPLETELY CHANGED MAN.

IT WAS THEN QUITE OBVIOUS THAT THERE WAS NO FUTURE FOR US IN GERMANY.

BRUSH BRUSH BRUSH

BRUSH BRUSH

THERE WAS NOWHERE FOR US TO GO. NO COUNTRY WANTED US.

SWISH

SWISH SWISH

SWISH

FRANK, MY BROTHER, WAS IN LEEDS.

HE TRIED VERY HARD TO GET ME A TRAINEE POST AND FINALLY SUCCEEDED...

Hamburg

Leeds

GREAT BRITAIN

...AND I CAME TO LEEDS.

GERMANY

DEUTSCHES REICH
J REISEPASS

DEUTSCHES REICH
J REISEPASS

BANG!

BANG!

BOOM! BOOM!

...WAR BROKE OUT.

BOOM!

WE MANAGED TO GET VISAS FOR OUR PARENTS EVENTUALLY. AND THEY CAME, THANK GOD, BECAUSE FOUR DAYS LATER...

THE DAY WAR BROKE OUT, A POLICEMAN CAME, ASKING US TO COME DOWN AND REPORT TO POLICE HEADQUARTERS.

I WAS REGISTERED AS AN...

ENEMY ALIEN

CAMERAS AND BINOCULARS WERE IMPOUNDED. THEY WERE CONSIDERED SPYING EQUIPMENT.

EIGHT MONTHS LATER, WINSTON CHURCHILL BECAME PRIME MINISTER AND HIS CIVIL SERVANTS FAMOUSLY ASKED HIM,

What shall we do with these enemy aliens?

Collar the lot!

SO WE WERE INTERNED, FATHER, BROTHER, AND ME.

BANG!

BANG!

BANG!

ALL OF US FELT A BIT ANGRY, BECAUSE WE WERE MORE OPPOSED TO THE NAZIS THAN THE NATIVE BRITISH WERE.

HEINZ AND HIS BROTHER FRANK WERE SENT TO INTERNMENT CAMPS IN CANADA FOR TWO YEARS. THEY NEVER DID GET THEIR CHANCE TO FIGHT THE NAZIS.

TRUDE'S STORY

ONE AND A HALF MILLION INNOCENT CHILDREN
WERE KILLED DURING THE HOLOCAUST.

AND WHEN
I LOOK AT
THESE FACES,
I DON'T
KNOW WHO
SURVIVED AND
WHO DIDN'T.

I ONLY
KNOW
THAT I
SURVIVED.

WHY SHOULD INNOCENT PEOPLE, JUST BECAUSE THEY WERE JEWISH,
BE KILLED FOR NO REASON AT ALL?

WE HAD THIS RADIO IN OUR DINING ROOM, AND FATHER WAS OFTEN LISTENING.

BUT WHEN HE HAD THE NEWS ON, YOU COULD HEAR THIS SHOUTING.

@!!*#

AND THAT, OF COURSE, WAS THE TYPICAL HITLER SPEECH-MAKING.

!%#!!!@

STOMP   STOMP   STOMP   STOMP   STOMP

THE GERMANS DIDN'T COME INTO CZECHOSLOVAKIA UNTIL MARCH 15TH, 1939.

BOOM!

I REALIZED THAT MY PARENTS WANTED TO GET THE OTHER CHILDREN AWAY TO SAFETY.

THEN MY TURN CAME. I LEFT HOME ON MARCH 28TH, 1939.

...B) I DIDN'T SPEAK ONE WORD OF ENGLISH.

THE FOOD WAS TOTALLY DIFFERENT. I'D NEVER EATEN TOAST, PORRIDGE, KIPPERS, MARMALADE...ALL OF THESE NORMAL ENGLISH THINGS.

AND I JUST BASICALLY CRIED FOR AS LONG AS I STAYED WITH THEM.

SOON, I MOVED ON. FROM THE AGE OF NINE, I LIVED WITH SO MANY DIFFERENT PEOPLE.

IN THOSE FOUR YEARS, IN THOSE WAR YEARS, I WOULD THINK I MUST HAVE BEEN THROUGH AT LEAST 15 TO 20 DIFFERENT PLACES.

I NEVER SAW MY PARENTS AFTER MARCH 28TH, 1939.

THE LAST PROPER EVIDENCE I HAVE THAT MY MOTHER WAS ALIVE...

...WAS WHEN SHE WAS TRANSPORTED TO A SMALL CONCENTRATION CAMP NEAR BRATISLAVA CALLED SERED.

AND I'VE BEEN WORKING FOR YEARS AND YEARS TO TRY AND TRACE HER...

...AND I'M ALMOST AT THE END OF THE TRAIL.

I RECEIVED SOME EVIDENCE FROM A TESTIMONY GIVEN BY SOMEBODY IN 1962...

...WHO COULD HAVE BEEN ON THE SAME TRANSPORT THAT MY MOTHER WAS TAKEN ON...

...AND ON A DEATH MARCH ON WHICH SHE WOULD HAVE BEEN SHOT AND KILLED.

THE IMPACT ON ME IS SOMETHING THAT HAS NEVER LEFT ME.

EVERY SINGLE DAY, I RUE THE DESTRUCTION OF MY FAMILY.

TO ME, FAMILY IS THE MOST IMPORTANT BUILDING BLOCK FOR HUMAN BEINGS...

...AND THAT'S WHY I FIND IT SO HARD TODAY.

TRUDE EVENTUALLY SETTLED WELL IN A BOARDING SCHOOL IN CORNWALL. SHE STUDIED HARD AND WENT ON TO UNIVERSITY.

RUTH'S STORY

I WAS BORN IN ZWICKAU, WHICH IS IN EASTERN GERMANY.

THERE'S QUITE A BIG MOUNTAIN RANGE THAT SEPARATED GERMANY FROM CZECHOSLOVAKIA.

THESE ARE CALLED THE ERZGEBIRGE, THE ORE MOUNTAINS.

MY FATHER WAS IN TROUBLE WITH THE NAZIS. HE TOOK US ALL OVER THE MOUNTAINS, LEAVING EVERYTHING BEHIND, AND WENT TO PRAGUE.

BUT HITLER MARCHED INTO PRAGUE IN MARCH 1939.

MY FATHER REALIZED HE WAS STILL ON A NAZI WANTED LIST...

...SO HE LEFT MY MOTHER AND WENT TO POLAND.

IT WAS EXTREMELY DIFFICULT FOR MY MOTHER TO BE LEFT ALONE WITH TWO SMALL CHILDREN.

SPLAT

STREET BY STREET, JEWS WERE CLEARED...

...AND ANY MOMENT IT WAS PROBABLY OUR TURN.

MY MOTHER...SHE MUST HAVE HAD A WILL OF IRON AND GREAT COURAGE.

SHE WENT FROM ONE EMBASSY TO ANOTHER TRYING TO ESCAPE THE NAZIS. SHE WAITED IN LINE ALL NIGHT...

...AND IF SHE EVER GOT TO THE DESK, THEY SAID TO HER,

We will take you, but we can't take your two children!

BUT MY MOTHER WOULDN'T SEPARATE US, SO SHE HUNG ON TO US.

THE ONLY THING SHE COULD THINK OF WAS TO HOPE THAT SOMEBODY WOULD TAKE HER AND THE CHILDREN.

SHE WAS REJECTED BY EVERYONE.

A KNOCK ON THE DOOR MEANT DEATH, BECAUSE IT MEANT DEPORTATION.

BUT FOR US A KNOCK ON THE DOOR WAS THE BEGINNING OF A NEW LIFE...

...BECAUSE WE OPENED THE DOOR TO A WOMAN FROM THE BRITISH EMBASSY WHO HAD BRAVED THE CURFEW.

WE MADE IT THROUGH CZECHOSLOVAKIA WITHOUT ANY PROBLEM, AND WE GOT ON THE TRAIN IN GERMANY.

WE SAT DOWN, THINKING,

Good, we've got a carriage to ourselves.

THEN A NAZI SS OFFICER CAME AND SAT NEXT TO MY MOTHER. HE WAS TRYING TO FLIRT WITH HER.

THE FACT THAT HE SAT THERE...NOW THAT MIGHT HAVE BEEN HER SALVATION, AS THE GUARDS DIDN'T ASK FOR HER PAPERS.

THE NEXT MORNING WAS SUNDAY, SEPTEMBER 3RD, 1939.

AS WE ARRIVED AT LIVERPOOL STREET STATION...

...I PUT MY FOOT ON THE PLATFORM.

SUDDENLY, EVERYTHING WENT QUIET AND THERE WAS AN ANNOUNCEMENT ON THE LOUDSPEAKER.

AND EVERYBODY STOOD PERFECTLY STILL.

THAT WAS 11 O'CLOCK, SEPTEMBER 3RD, 1939, AS MY FOOT HIT THE PLATFORM.

AND THAT WAS THE BEGINNING OF THE SECOND WORLD WAR.

RUTH'S WHOLE FAMILY WAS REUNITED SHORTLY AFTER THEIR ARRIVAL IN LONDON. THEY WERE LUCKY TO BE ALIVE.

MARTIN'S STORY

IN 1938, WHEN I WAS EIGHT YEARS OLD...

...THERE OCCURRED WHAT HAS BECOME KNOWN AS THE "POLENAKTION."

POLAND

EARLY IN THE MORNING, WE WERE ALL SLEEPING IN OUR BEDS IN OUR HOME IN GERMANY. THE NAZIS ENTERED OUR FLAT.

WE WERE GOING TO BE TAKEN AWAY.

WE WERE PUT ON BOARD A TRAIN.

WE CAME TO REALIZE THAT THE PASSENGERS WERE ALL POLISH JEWS.

WE WERE LUCKIER THAN SOME. WE HAD BEEN TAKEN AS AN ENTIRE FAMILY.

SOME OF THE FAMILIES HAD BEEN SEPARATED. THEY DIDN'T KNOW WHETHER THEY WERE EVER GOING TO SEE ONE ANOTHER EVER AGAIN.

TO MAKE MATTERS WORSE, THERE WERE PEOPLE OF ALL AGES...

WAAA!

...BABIES...

...THERE WERE VERY OLD PEOPLE...

AND PEOPLE WHO WERE ILL. SOME HAD BEEN TAKEN OUT OF HOSPITAL BEDS.

I SAW PEOPLE COLLAPSE FROM EXHAUSTION, AND I WAS LEFT IN NO DOUBT ABOUT THE BRUTALITY OF THESE SS MEN.

WE MARCHED FOR HOURS....

...AND THEN WE WERE STOPPED AT A RAILWAY LINE, AND WE WERE TOLD THAT THE SS MEN WERE NOT COMING ANY FARTHER.

THE POLISH AUTHORITIES DID TRY TO FORCE SOME PEOPLE BACK INTO GERMANY.

GERMANY

POLAND

THE GERMAN AUTHORITIES WERE READY FOR THAT, AND POLISH ATTEMPTS TO SEND PEOPLE BACK TO GERMANY FAILED.

BUT WE MANAGED TO GET TO KRAKÓW IN POLAND WHERE WE HAD SOME RELATIVES...

...AND WE ARRIVED ON THEIR DOORSTEP.

ABOUT THE TIME THAT WE WENT TO POLAND, BRITAIN ALLOWED SOME JEWISH CHILDREN TO BE BROUGHT OVER FROM EUROPE, IN WHAT BECAME KNOWN AS THE "KINDERTRANSPORT."

MY SISTER AND I WERE VERY LUCKY TO BE AMONG THE FEW CHILDREN TO BE RESCUED FROM POLAND.

...y is issued with the approval of His Majesty's Government ...in the United Kingdom to your... ...to be admitted to the United Kingdom for educational purposes un... ...Inter-Aid Committee for children.

THIS DO... ...RES NO VISA.

PL... ...ULARS.

Name Martin Kap...
Sex Male
Place Leipzig, G...

WE WOULD HAVE DIED WITH THE REST OF OUR FAMILY IF WE HADN'T BEEN RESCUED.

WE WENT TO FOSTER PARENTS IN COVENTRY IN ENGLAND.

IN THE AUTUMN OF 1940, THE SO-CALLED BLITZ BEGAN.

COVENTRY WAS ONE OF THE MOST SEVERELY BOMBED CITIES.

WE HAD 17 RAIDS WHEN A FEW BOMBS WERE DROPPED ON THE CITY.

AND THEN ONE NIGHT, WE HAD A VERY BIG RAID.

THE HOME OFFICE ADVICE WAS THAT IF YOU DIDN'T HAVE AN AIR-RAID SHELTER, THE SAFEST PART OF THE HOUSE WAS UNDER THE STAIRS.

UNDER OUR STAIRS WE HAD A SMALL PANTRY, SO WE ALL CROWDED INTO THAT, MY SISTER AND I...

...OUR FOSTER PARENTS...

...AND THE DOG.

THE DOG WAS VICIOUS. HE BIT QUITE A FEW PEOPLE. WE TRIED TO KEEP OUR DISTANCE.

BUT WHENEVER A BOMB CAME VERY NEAR, THE DOG GROWLED AND WE WERE REALLY AFRAID, ALL OF US.

THE NEXT MORNING, WHEN WE EMERGED, OUR HOUSE HAD LOST ITS DOORS AND ITS WINDOWS AND PART OF THE ROOF.

IT'S AMAZING THAT THERE WERE MANY SMALL AIR RAIDS...

ICES 1½ 2

CARROTS 1D. each

...AND GENERALLY SPEAKING, PEOPLE TOOK THEM IN STRIDE.

BUT DURING THOSE BIG AIR RAIDS...

...I CERTAINLY FELT VERY MUCH AFRAID.

AND I DON'T THINK VERY MANY PEOPLE, IF THEY ARE TRUTHFUL, COULD SAY OTHERWISE.

BOTH MARTIN AND HIS SISTER SURVIVED THE BOMBINGS IN COVENTRY, AND SETTLED WELL INTO THEIR NEW LIVES IN ENGLAND.

SUZANNE'S STORY

SLOWLY, SLOWLY, MY LIFE CHANGED.

THE FIRST THING WE COULDN'T DO WAS WE COULDN'T GO OUT.

YOU STARTED TO HEAR NOISES THAT YOU HADN'T HEARD BEFORE. IT WAS REALLY SCARY SOMETIMES.

AS I UNDERSTAND IT NOW, WE WERE OCCUPIED, AND ALL OF THE SHOUTING AND ACTIVITY YOU COULD HEAR OUTSIDE WERE NAZI SOLDIERS.

THE DAY IT HAPPENED, IT WAS AUGUST AND IT WAS HOT.

I WAS WITH MY FATHER AT THE WINDOW, AND SUDDENLY HE SAID,

They're here!

DURING ALL THE COMMOTION, MADAME COLLOMB CAME IN.

SHE WAS OUR NEXT-DOOR NEIGHBOR.

What's my child doing in this apartment?

SHE TOOK MY HAND, AND TOOK ME AWAY.

HAD THEY REALIZED WHAT SHE WAS DOING, WE'D HAVE ALL BEEN SHOT ON THE SPOT. BUT SHE GOT AWAY WITH IT.

SHE TOOK ME TO HER APARTMENT AND PUT ME UNDERNEATH HER DINING TABLE, WITH A BIG CHENILLE TABLECLOTH OVER IT.

SHE MADE ME A LITTLE BED, AND I LIVED THERE FOR TWO OR THREE WEEKS.

IT WAS SOLITARY, AND IT WAS LONELY AND IT WAS DARK.

I HAD NIGHTMARES THERE.

I NEVER SAW MY PARENTS AGAIN AFTER THAT.

AND I WAS LOST, A TOTALLY LOST CHILD.

AFTER THAT, MADAME COLLOMB TOOK ME OUT ONE NIGHT, AND FURTIVELY WE HAD TO GO CATCH A TRAIN.

THE FIRST HIDING PLACE SHE TOOK ME TO WAS MONDOUBLEAU, WHICH IS SOUTHWEST OF PARIS.

MONDOUBLEAU

I COULDN'T GO TO SCHOOL.
I COULDN'T GO OUT ON THE STREET
BECAUSE THERE WERE GERMAN SOLDIERS EVERYWHERE.

I SLEPT OCCASIONALLY INSIDE THE HOUSE...

SPLASH

SPLASH

...BUT THEN OTHER TIMES I WENT AND SLEPT WITH THE GOAT...

...BECAUSE SHE'D HAD SOME KIDS.

THEY WERE WARM AND THEY WERE FRIENDLY AND THEY WOULD SNUFFLE AGAINST YOUR CHEEK.

THE WAR ENDED IN 1945,
AND I WAS STILL IN THE AUVERGNE FOR TWO YEARS.
WE DIDN'T KNOW. WE HADN'T BEEN TOLD.

I DIDN'T KNOW
THE WAR WAS
OVER,
BECAUSE WE
DIDN'T HAVE
NEWSPAPERS.

WE DIDN'T
HAVE A
RADIO, WE
DIDN'T HAVE
ELECTRICITY,
NOBODY
KNEW.

SUZANNE WAS EVENTUALLY RESCUED BY THE RED CROSS AND
TAKEN TO LIVE WITH HER GRANDMOTHER IN NEWCASTLE, ENGLAND.

AREK'S STORY

I WAS BORN IN SIERADZ IN POLAND. ONE DAY, WHEN I WAS 15, THE NAZIS CAME AND TOOK US AWAY.

IN THE WAGON THERE WAS ONLY ONE VERY SMALL WINDOW.

IT WAS HOT.

WE WERE SO CRAMPED...

I'm so thirsty!

...WE COULDN'T EVEN SIT DOWN.

AAAHHH!!

SOME PEOPLE HAD SOME WATER, AND SOME PEOPLE DIDN'T.

WE HAD ARRIVED IN
BIRKENAU, AUSCHWITZ.

I'D NOTICED A LOT OF THE PEOPLE WHO WERE CHOSEN TO GO TO THE RIGHT WERE FITTER MEN.

I KNEW THAT WAS A GOOD THING WITH THE NAZIS.

IF THEY DIDN'T NEED YOU, THEN THAT WAS IT.

AAHHH!

THEN SUDDENLY, THEY TRIED TO TAKE A CHILD AWAY FROM HER MOTHER.

My daughter!

AND SHE STARTED SCREAMING, AND THE NAZI SS MEN RAN TOWARD HER.

AS THEY RAN THERE, I DECIDED TO GO OVER TO THE RIGHT.

I WAS VERY LUCKY. ALL THE PEOPLE THAT WENT TO THE LEFT-HAND SIDE WENT TO THE GAS CHAMBERS. THEY GASSED THEM AND THEN BURNED THEIR BODIES.

WE WALKED INTO A PLACE CALLED THE SAUNA...

...A BRICK-BUILT BUILDING IN BIRKENAU.

WE WERE TOLD TO LEAVE ALL OUR CLOTHING ON THE FLOOR.

I HAD SIX PHOTOGRAPHS OF MY FAMILY...

THEY WERE TAKEN AWAY, AND THAT'S THE LAST TIME I'VE EVER HAD A PHOTOGRAPH OF MY FAMILY.

I HAD MY HEAD SHAVED.

AND FROM THERE, WE WENT INTO THE NEXT ROOM AND WERE GIVEN OUR UNIFORMS.

STRIPED SUITS. MINE WAS BIG ON ME, SO I PULLED IT UP.

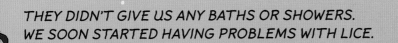
THEY DIDN'T GIVE US ANY BATHS OR SHOWERS.
WE SOON STARTED HAVING PROBLEMS WITH LICE.

LICE WALKED ALL OVER US. ITCHY, YES, VERY ITCHY. THEY LIVE ON YOUR SKIN.

WE WERE A THOUSAND MEN IN A BARRACK.

THREE BUNKS HIGH...

...TEN PEOPLE ON A BUNK.

WE SLEPT ON THE BOARDS. THERE WAS NO STRAW, THERE WERE NO COVERS.

PEOPLE SNORED, PEOPLE MOANED, PEOPLE DIED NEXT TO YOU.

AT 5:30 IN THE MORNING, THEY WOKE US UP AND THEY ALLOWED US TO GO TO THE WASHROOM.

DING

DING

IN THE WASHROOM THERE WERE ABOUT FIVE BUCKETS OF WATER.

AND YOU JUST DIPPED YOUR HANDS...

...WASHED YOUR EYES...

...AND THAT WAS IT.

I WAS JUST SKIN AND BONES, BECAUSE THEY DIDN'T FEED US.

I'm so hungry!

THEY GAVE US A SMALL PIECE OF BREAD IN THE MORNING, WITH SOME BLACK COFFEE MADE OF BURNT WHEAT.

IN AUSCHWITZ, I WAS TATTOOED. I'VE GOT A NUMBER...

B7608

...ON MY LEFT ARM. IT'S STILL THERE NOW, AND I JUST CAN'T TAKE IT OFF.

I'VE LOST 81 PEOPLE FROM MY FAMILY.

I ONLY FOUND MY SISTER TWO YEARS AFTER THE WAR.

HOW COULD I SAY HOW IT CHANGED ME?

SPLASH SPLASH SPLASH

I'LL NEVER FORGET WHAT I WENT THROUGH.

I SUFFERED SO MUCH.

IT WAS THE MOST HORRIFIC THING ANY HUMAN BEING COULD EVER SEE.

THE WORLD SHOULD NEVER SEE THAT AGAIN.

AREK SURVIVED SEVERAL GHETTOS AND CONCENTRATION CAMPS BETWEEN THE AGES OF 11 AND 16. ONLY 40 PEOPLE FROM AREK'S HOMETOWN SURVIVED THE WAR.

What Happened Next?

HEINZ

After the war ended, Heinz married Thea. They had two sons. Both sons went to Oxford, the first members of the family ever to go to college. Heinz had a successful career as head of a leading housing organization.

TRUDE

Trude did very well at school and won a scholarship to college. She went on to become a medical biochemist and university lecturer. Trude is still searching for information about what happened to her mother.

RUTH

Ruth married, had five children, and became a successful secondary school teacher. She continues to speak about her experiences in schools in England and in Israel, and is committed to keeping the memory of the Holocaust alive.

MARTIN

Martin's mother and sister also survived the war. None of Martin's relatives in Poland were so fortunate—22 of them in total were rounded up and shot by the Nazis. Martin went on to become an eminent scientist and a university lecturer.

SUZANNE

It took Suzanne many years to learn and understand what happened to her during the war. She now has two sons and several grandchildren. Madame Collomb, Suzanne's rescuer, has been recognized for her bravery at the Yad Vashem Holocaust Museum in Israel.

AREK

Many years passed before Arek could talk fully about his experiences of the war. He subsequently wrote a book about what happened. Today he gives talks and shows groups around Auschwitz-Birkenau. He has been given an award by Queen Elizabeth II for his work.

Glossary

air-raid shelter *The place where people hide from bombs being dropped from airplanes.*

arrondissement *An administrative district (neighborhood) of certain large cities in France, including Paris.*

barracks *A building or group of buildings used as basic living quarters.*

Blitz *A period of intense German air raids on British cities, from September 1940 to May 1941.*

British Ambassador *The head of the British Embassy, who represents his or her government in a foreign country.*

chenille *Thick cloth.*

civil servant *Someone who works in a government office.*

concentration camps *Purpose-built camps used by the Nazis to imprison huge numbers of Jewish people, as well as others including communists, homosexuals, and church leaders.*

curfew *The time period when people have to stay indoors or risk breaking the law.*

Czechoslovakia *A country that used to exist in eastern Europe and which was divided into the Czech Republic and Slovakia in 1993.*

deportation *Being forced to leave your home and your country.*

digs *Rented room or rooms to live in.*

embassy *The building where an ambassador and his officials live and work in a foreign country.*

enemy aliens *Foreigners who were living in Britain when the Second World War broke out and who came from countries that were now at war with Britain.*

foster parents *People who act as a child's parents in place of their own parents.*

gas chamber *An airtight room that can be filled with poisonous gas in order to poison the people inside.*

Gestapo *Secret police who played a large role in persecuting Jewish people.*

ghettos *Overcrowded districts within cities, designed to separate Jewish people from the rest of the population.*

Hitler, Adolf (1889–1945) *The political leader of Germany from 1933 to 1945 and the head of the Nazi Party.*

Hitler Youth *German youth group, controlled by the Nazi Party.*

Holocaust *The systematic murder of six million Jewish people by the Nazi Party.*

Home Office *The part of the British government responsible for law and order, security, and immigration.*

inferior *Feeling that you are not as good as someone else.*

internment camp *A camp where enemy aliens were kept captive for political reasons.*

Jew *A member of the Jewish community who may also follow the religion Judaism.*

Jude *The German word for a Jewish person.*

Kindertransport (Children's Transport) The name given to the rescue efforts that brought approximately 10,000 children to Great Britain as refugees from Nazi persecution between 1938 and 1940.

kipper A smoked herring; a type of fish.

Kristallnacht The anti-Jewish riots that occurred on November 9th and 10th, 1938. Thousands of Jews were arrested and their homes, synagogues, and businesses were burnt down or wrecked.

marionettes Puppets whose legs, feet, and head are moved by pulling on strings.

Mengele, Dr. Josef (1911–1979) Nazi doctor, member of the SS, who worked at Auschwitz-Birkenau, performing cruel operations and other medical procedures as part of his medical research.

Nazis Short for the National Socialist German Workers' (Nazi) Party. This was a German political party that existed from 1920 to 1945.

Nuremberg Laws Laws passed by the Nazi Party in 1935 that stripped Jewish people of German citizenship.

occupied/occupation From June 1940 to late August 1944, Germans governed (occupied) northern and western France, including Paris.

pantry A cupboard or small room in a house used for storing food.

peers People of the same age.

Polenaktion In October 1938, 12,000 Polish Jews living in Germany were deported—expelled—from Germany.

Red Cross An international organization that cares for people suffering because of war or natural disasters.

Reisepass The German word for passport.

salvation Being saved from danger.

selection platform New arrivals at concentration camps were processed by officials standing on a raised platform and were selected to die immediately or be sent to work.

self-sufficient Being able to provide for all your needs and not rely on help from anyone else.

SS Short for Schutzstaffel, the German word for defense squadron. This military unit of the Nazi Party served as Adolf Hitler's bodyguards and became a major security force for the Nazi Party in concentration camps.

Star of David A six-pointed star that is a symbol of the Jewish religion.

swastika An ancient symbol that was used by the German Nazi Party.

synagogue Jewish place of worship.

testimony A spoken statement, often in a court of law, saying what someone believes to be true.

transport/transported The term used to describe rounding up Jewish people and putting them on trains to travel to concentration camps, death camps, and work camps.

visa An official stamp or mark put into a passport by a government official which gives someone the right to enter a foreign country or leave their own country.

Timeline

January 30, 1933
Adolf Hitler is appointed Chancellor, the German head of government. He leads the National Socialist German Workers'(Nazi) Party.

March 1933
The Nazis open the first concentration camps where they imprison anyone who opposes their ideas.

1933–1935
The German government gradually introduces laws that isolate Jewish people from the rest of society and limit their freedom and opportunities. They use propaganda, such as speeches and newspaper articles, to spread lies about Jewish people, burn books by Jewish authors, and encourage people to boycott Jewish shops and businesses. Jewish people are banned from mixing with non-Jewish people in parks, swimming pools, orchestras, clubs, and playgrounds. Many Jewish children and students are forced to leave school or university.

September 15, 1935
The Nuremberg Laws take away German citizenship from Jews.

March 13, 1938
German troops march into Austria.

October 1938
Polenaktion: 12,000 Polish Jews living in Germany are deported (expelled) from Germany.

November 9–10, 1938
Kristallnacht: Anti-Jewish riots occur throughout Germany, Austria, and Sudetenland (disputed land in Czechoslovakia). Synagogues, Jewish homes, and businesses are destroyed by fire or have their windows smashed. Thousands of Jewish people are arrested and kept in camps for several weeks and others are murdered. Life for Jewish people becomes considerably more difficult.

November/December 1938
Jewish children are only allowed to attend separate Jewish schools.

December 1938–1940
Kindertransport rescue missions bring 10,000 Jewish children to Britain. The children have to be under 17 years old, travel without their parents, and have arrangements in place where either individuals or organizations are prepared to pay for their needs in Great Britain.

March 15, 1939
Germany invades Czechoslovakia.

September 1, 1939
Germany invades Poland.

September 3, 1939
Britain and France declare war on Germany. Prime Minister Neville Chamberlain announces that Britain is at war with Germany using a radio broadcast. Enemy aliens are put in internment camps or placed under surveillance.

September 17, 1939
The Soviet Union invades Poland. By the end of the month, Germany and the Soviet Union have divided Poland between themselves.

September 21, 1939
From this date, Polish Jews are ordered to live in ghettos.

October 1939
The Nazis begin to deport Jewish people from Austria and Poland to camps.

November 1939
Polish Jews are forced to wear a Star of David on their chests or as an armband.

1940
Prime Minister Neville Chamberlain resigns, to be replaced by Winston Churchill.

1940
In Germany, Jewish people have their telephones removed; they had already had their radios confiscated in 1939.

April 30, 1940
The Lodz ghetto in Poland is the first ghetto to be sealed off behind guarded defenses.

April–June 1940
Germany invades Denmark, Norway, Luxembourg, the Netherlands, and Belgium. France signs an armistice agreement whereby the Germans occupy the northern half of the country, including Paris, and southern France is governed by the Vichy French government.

July 1940
French Jews are expelled to southern France.

September 1940–May 1941
The Blitz: a succession of intense bombing raids by the German air force on British cities, including London and Coventry.

1941
Jewish people are forbidden from using public telephones or leaving the country. Jewish people from across German-occupied territory are forcibly removed to ghettos or camps.

June 1941
Germany invades the Soviet Union. German troops are ordered to kill all Jewish people they come across.

September 1941
All Jewish people over the age of 6 have to wear a yellow Star of David with "Jew" written on it.

December 1941
Japan attacks Pearl Harbor, leading to the U.S. declaring war against Germany, Japan, and Italy.

1941–1942
The Nazis open six extermination or death camps in Poland, including Auschwitz-Birkenau.

January 1942
Nazi leaders meet in Berlin to discuss how to organize the mass murder of the Jewish people, known as the "Final Solution."

February 1942
Gas chambers begin operation at Auschwitz-Birkenau, murdering Jewish people.

June 1942
The German government closes all Jewish schools.

July 1942
Around 74,000 French Jews are transported to death camps.

1942–1943
German forces deport Jewish people from ghettos to camps, where thousands are forced into gas chambers and killed, or worked to death in forced labor camps.

May 1943
Dr. Mengele begins work at Auschwitz-Birkenau.

May–July 1944
Jews are deported from Hungary to camps, such as Auschwitz-Birkenau.

June 6, 1944
D-Day: U.S., British, Canadian, and French forces (and other Allied troops) invade German-held Normandy in France. Slowly they fight their way across Europe.

June 22, 1944
The Soviet Union launches a major attack on German forces in eastern Europe and pushes across Poland, uncovering evidence of many concentration camps.

Late 1944–spring 1945
As the German army retreats from the Soviet army, the SS forces prisoners in concentration camps to march west, sometimes traveling in train carriages, back to Germany. Known as "death marches," hundreds of thousands of Jewish people die.

January 1945
Soviet troops liberate prisoners remaining in Auschwitz-Birkenau.

1945
As British and U.S. troops and those fighting alongside them fight their way across Europe and into Germany, they come across horribly overcrowded camps, full of prisoners on the verge of death. Many prisoners are so weak that they die.

April 30, 1945
Adolf Hitler commits suicide.

May 8, 1945
Victory in Europe (VE) Day. Germany surrenders and the Second World War in Europe comes to an end.

Summer 1945 onward
Displaced persons camps are established across Austria, Italy, and Germany for people rescued from Nazi camps and other refugees. At first, conditions are poor, but gradually they improve and aid agencies help people to trace surviving relatives and start to rebuild their lives.

August 1945
Atomic bombs are dropped on Hiroshima and Nagasaki in Japan, killing between 150,000–300,000 people. Japan surrenders and the Second World War comes to an end.

Index

Websites

BBC Learning Children of the Holocaust animations
Watch the animations that inspired this book, and interviews with the survivors themselves.
bbc.co.uk/programmes/po1zx5g7

Fettle Animation
The multi-award-winning animation company behind this project.
fettleanimation.com

Holocaust Survivors' Friendship Association
Find out more about the people in this book and their ongoing educational work.
holocaustlearning.org

6 Million Plus
Organization in Yorkshire, UK, that explores the connection between the Holocaust and the experience of persecuted minorities today.
6millionplus.org

Holocaust Memorial Day Trust
The charity that promotes and supports Holocaust Memorial Day on January 27th every year.
hmd.org.uk

The National Holocaust Centre and Museum
Museum in Nottingham, UK, that hosts daily talks by Holocaust survivors, plus an exhibition designed especially for younger children.
nationalholocaustcentre.net

Anne Frank Trust
Resources to help children understand the Holocaust.
annefrank.org.uk

Imperial War Museum London
Award-winning permanent Holocaust exhibition.
iwm.org.uk/events/the-holocaust-exhibition

Yad Vashem
Museum and Holocaust research institute in Israel.
yadvashem.org

Wiener Library London
Library for the study of the Holocaust and genocide.
wienerlibrary.co.uk

International Tracing Service
Center for research on the Holocaust, documenting what happened to victims of the Nazis.
its-arolsen.org

USC Shoah Foundation
Archive of interviews with Holocaust survivors and educational resources.
sfi.usc.edu

United States Holocaust Memorial Museum
U.S. memorial to the Holocaust. Features an exhibition designed for young people and a Hall of Remembrance.
ushmm.org

Auschwitz-Birkenau Memorial and Museum
Visit the former concentration camp and tour its museum.
auschwitz.org/en/